The Solar System

THE Moon

Núria Roca & Carol Isern
Rocio Bonilla

BARRON'S

Is it magic?

Today, the Moon seems to have disappeared from the sky. The night has become very dark. "It seems like magic, doesn't it?" laughs Alice's mother.

But it isn't magic, it's a lunar eclipse. Scientists have studied eclipses very well; they can even predict them!

A matter of science

Scientists discovered that the Earth positions itself between the Moon and the Sun. That's why the Earth blocks the sunlight from getting to the Moon, which prevents us from seeing it.

Not all eclipses are the same. Sometimes the whole Moon is covered and other times only part of it is covered. But, they are always spectacular!

Eclipses are very old

We have known about eclipses for many, many years.
Even the Assyrians and the Babylonians studied them.

Today, we can predict eclipses by using computers to calculate the movements of the Earth and the Moon.

The Moon plays hide-and-seek

"And when the Moon is shaped like an orange slice, is that a half eclipse?" asks Oliver. "Nooo!" replies Alice's mother.

Sometimes the Moon appears very round, other times it looks like a very thin "C," and other times you can't see it at all. These are the different phases of the Moon.

The phases of the Moon

Scientists have determined four phases of the Moon:
Full, waxing, waning, and new.

In the full moon phase, the Moon appears large and round.
In the waxing phase, the Moon is D-shaped. In the waning
phase, it is C-shaped. And when you can't see it at all,
it is the new moon.

Shadows on the Moon

Alice's mother has given them some binoculars so that they can look at the Moon. "Wow! It's full of craters and mountains!" exclaims Oliver.

The Moon doesn't have light of its own.
It reflects the light from the Sun like
a mirror. That's why you need binoculars
with special filters, so that it doesn't
damage your eyes!

The Moon has a face

When you look at the Moon, it looks like it has a face, doesn't it? This is the effect produced by the shadows of its craters and mountains.

That's why the Moon is often drawn with a face.

The Moon is our companion

The Moon is the closest astral body in the solar system to the Earth. It always accompanies us, because it's our satellite. A satellite is an astral body that revolves around a planet.

But the Earth is much larger. If the Earth were the size of a grape, the Moon would be… "Like the size of a pea!" says Alice.

Mercury and Venus are alone

The Earth is not the only planet with a satellite; many neighboring planets also have them.

The Earth only has one. Mars has two. Saturn, Jupiter, Uranus, and Neptune have many. And Mercury and Venus don't have any at all.

The Sea of Tranquility

"There were once some intrepid explorers who traveled to the Moon. They were Michael Collins, Neil Armstrong, and Buzz Aldrin," says Alice's mother.

"Armstrong left a footprint on the ground of the Moon,
in a place called the Sea of Tranquility."

There are no seas on the Moon

"Are there any seas on the Moon?" asks Oliver.

"No, but this name was given to an expanse that is as large as a sea. There are no rivers, or trees, or animals, or traffic lights, or houses, or dogs, or cats. On the Moon, there is only very fine dust that doesn't move because there is no wind!"

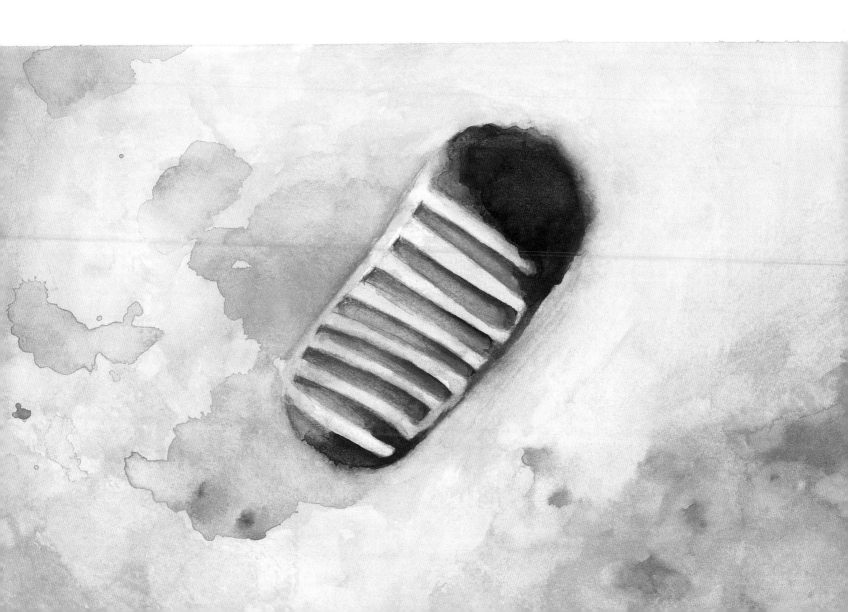

Meteorites and craters

"There are many large, deep craters on the Moon,"
says Alice's mother.

"Chunks of rock called meteorites travel through the sky. When they fall on the surface of the Moon, some of these meteorites form enormous holes called craters."

You cannot live on the Moon

If you went to the Moon, you would always see the sky black and full of stars. During the day it is almost as hot as the inside of an oven, and at night it is colder than the inside of a freezer.

"That's why we couldn't live there. Besides, there is no water," says Alice's mother.

Armstrong's jump

"I would like to jump around on the Moon just like Armstrong!" says Oliver, who has seen some videos.

Armstrong jumped because there isn't much gravity on the Moon. If you tried to walk there, you would jump, too! You would jump so high that you would look like an athlete!

Earth, the blue planet

The explorers who went to the Moon took a photograph that has become famous and shows the Earth floating in space.

The Earth is called the blue planet because it looks like a giant blue ball due to the seas. There are also white swirls because of clouds, ice, and snow.

Activities

A plate full of craters

Ask a grown-up to help you with this activity in the kitchen. You will need a plate, a packet of flour, and some rice. Pour the flour onto the plate until you have a layer about ½ inch (1 cm) thick. Now you're ready to start! Throw grains of rice into the flour and watch different-sized craters form. The harder you throw the grains of rice, the larger the craters will be.

How much slower do objects fall on the Moon?

The Moon has less gravity than the Earth. Less gravity will make objects fall slower. Here's an activity to show the difference.

Take an object, such as a ball or a pencil. Ask a grown-up to help you climb onto a chair. Next, drop the object and count how many seconds it takes for the object to fall from your hand to the floor. You can count the seconds by saying "one one thousand, two one thousand, three one thousand." Once you know the amount of time it takes for the object to fall on Earth, find out how much longer it would take to fall on the Moon by multiplying the number of seconds by 6.

For example, if something takes 2 seconds to fall on Earth, it would take 12 seconds on the Moon ($2 \times 6 = 12$). To see the difference, hold the object from the original starting height and slowly lower it, while you count up to 12 seconds. Do this with different objects to see how much longer they will take to fall on the Moon!

Parent's guide

After the Sun, the Moon is the object that shines the brightest in the sky. To observe the Moon, binoculars are very useful, but it's better to look at it after the full moon phase because the shadows make the image more interesting. Although looking at the Moon through binoculars is not as dangerous as observing the Sun, it is advisable to use moon filters for the UV rays that it reflects. These filters cannot be used for looking at the Sun.

The **phases of the Moon** are an illumination effect: Depending on where the Moon is in relation to the Sun and the Earth, it is seen illuminated in a different way. When the Sun illuminates the whole face you see, we say that it is full. When it does not illuminate it, we say that it is new. In the middle of these phases, we see a part that is growing or shrinking. In the northern hemisphere of the planet, when the Moon has a "C" shape, it is in the waning quarter; and when it has a "D" shape, it is in the waxing quarter.

In ancient times, time was already measured using the phases of the Moon. A phase lasts approximately one week, and the whole cycle lasts about a month.

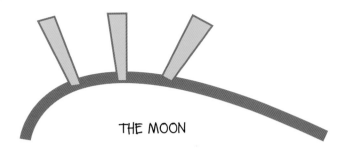

THE MOON

First edition for
North America published in 2014
by Barron's Educational Series, Inc.
© Gemser Publications, S.L. 2013
El Castell, 38 08329 Teià (Barcelona, Spain)
www.mercedesros.com
Text: Núria Roca and Carol Isern
Illustration: Rocio Bonilla
Design and layout: Estudi Guasch, S.L.

All inquiries should be addressed to:
Barron's Educational Series, Inc.
250 Wireless Boulevard
Hauppauge, NY 11788
www.barronseduc.com

ISBN: 978-1-4380-0476-1
Library of Congress Control Number: 2014935197

Date of Manufacture: June 2014
Manufactured by: L. Rex Printing Company Limited,
Dongguan City, Guangdong, China

Printed in China
9 8 7 6 5 4 3 2 1

A **lunar eclipse** occurs when the Earth is positioned between the Sun and the Moon, that is, when the Earth casts a shadow on the Moon. But during an eclipse, the shadow of the Earth is not completely black, but rather a reddish tone because of the atmosphere, which gives color to the rays of sunlight that pass through it. This is why, during an eclipse, the Moon does not disappear from view when it is blackened, but rather acquires a reddish color instead of its usual luminous tone.

Apollo 11 was a lunar mission that took man to the Moon for the first time. Collins, Armstrong, and Aldrin traveled in the spaceship. While Collins, inside the spaceship was in charge of supervising the maneuvers of the lunar exploration module, Armstrong and Aldrin walked on the surface of the Moon. This took place on July 20, 1969. Armstrong said the famous sentence: "That's one small step for man, one giant leap for mankind." The event was broadcast on worldwide television.

Gravity is a force of attraction that exists between objects that have mass, that is, matter expressed in kilograms. The more mass an object has, the greater is its force of gravity. The planet Earth has a force of gravity that prevents us from flying off into space and enables us to walk on the ground with absolute tranquility. Given that the Moon is smaller than the Earth, it has a smaller mass and its gravity is less. That's why Armstrong jumped on the surface of the ground when he walked on it.